Syllables of Flesh

by Floarea Țuțuianu

Translated by Adam J. Sorkin and Irma Giannetti

Illustrations by Floarea Țuțuianu

Washington, DC

Plamen Press

9039 Sligo Creek Parkway

Silver Spring, MD 20901

www.plamenpress.com

Published by Plamen Press, 2017

Printed in the United States of America

10 9 8 7 6 5 4 3 2 1

LIBRARY OF CONGRESS CATALOGING-IN-PUBLICATION DATA

Ţuţuianu, Floarea

Syllables of Flesh: Floarea Ţuţuianu

p. cm.

ISBN: 978-0-9960722-3-6 (paperback)
ISBN: 978-1-951508-22-7 (EPUB)
ISBN: 978-1-951508-23-4 (PDF)
Library of Congress Control Number: 2017934260

Translated from Romanian by Adam J. Sorkin and Irma Giannetti

Edited by Rachel Miranda Feingold

Cover Art by Floarea Ţuţuianu
Cover Design by Roman Kostovski

Editors

Rachel Miranda Feingold

Roman Kostovski

Contents

Acknowledgments

The translators express gratitude to the editors of the following publications, in which some of the poems in this book appeared earlier: the literary journals *5 AM*, *Apostrof*, *Artful Dodge*, *Blood Orange Review*, *Caper Literary Journal*, *Diode*, *The Dirty Goat*, *Levure littéraire/Literary Yeast*, *The Marlboro Review*, *Modern Poetry in Translation*, *New Letters*, *Poetry International*, *Puerto del Sol*, *Respiro*, *The Saranac Review*, *St. Petersburg Review*, *Sleet Magazine*, *Tampa Review*, *Turnrow*; and the books *Arta seducției* by Floarea Țuțuianu (Bucharest: Editura Vinea, 2002); *The Vanishing Point That Whistles: An Anthology of Contemporary Romanian Poetry*, ed. Paul Doru Mugur, Adam J. Sorkin, and Claudia Serea (Greenfield, MA: Talisman House, 2011); *Romanian Writers on Writing*, ed. Norman Manea and Sanda Cordoș (San Antonio, TX: Trinity University Press, 2011); *My Dog – the Soul / Câinele meu – sufletul* (Governors Bay, New Zealand: Cold Hub Press, 2011); *Moods & Women & Men & Once Again Moods: An Anthology of Contemporary Romanian Erotic Poetry*, ed. Ruxandra Cesereanu (Bucharest: Tracus Arte/Calypso Editions, 2015).

Foreword

Floarea Țuțuianu: "Not my body, not my soul, but my sex at the word's heart"

Adam J. Sorkin

Floarea Țuțuianu (pronounced "Tsu-tsu-ya'-nu") writes fiercely sensual poetry. Her voice is as playful as it is provocative, seemingly confessional at times, and always intelligent. Her lyrical presence has an edgy quality, energized by the intrinsically ironic persona the reader discovers on her pages: those "paper children" the artist makes and nurtures, her power twice any man's, as she taunts the "men of paper" that she says she "invented." Țuțuianu's irony suggests a critical detachment and a duality of perspective: the image of her gendered self, both sensual and hyperbolic, accommodating and confronting—at moments, affronting—the external world. At its core, her work embodies the poet-as-woman in her yearning for an impossible intensity of experience, a mystical and sexual embrace of the world. This sensibility is at once erotic, feverish in its longing for unattainable fulfillment, and also metaphoric and thereby incomplete, a gesture of the aesthetic imagination. The projected identity of dust with dust, of word with world, turns back upon her narcissistically, as "flesh of my flesh/and blood of my blood," becomes a simulacrum for "soul." The metaphoric—a reaching out, ahead and beyond—thus transforms eroticism into a holy lust, an urgent need for the spiritual.

Beneath the self-mythologized Floarea Țuțuianu of the poems, the biographical human being is in fact a master of two arts. A graduate of the Nicolae Grigorescu Institute of the Fine Arts in Bucharest, she began to exhibit her drawings and paintings in 1980, and her visual art has been regularly presented to the public in group shows and single exhibitions in Poland, Israel, the U.S., Germany, England, and Italy, not to mention Romania. Currently, Ţuţuianu works as a graphic designer at the Romanian Cultural Institute Publishing House, also in Bucharest. As a writer she did not make her debut until the mid-1990s, with poetry in the major Romanian periodical *Literary Romania*. The first of her six collections, *The Fish Woman* (*Femeia peşte,* Editura Cartea Românească, 1996), came out a year later. Three other books followed within half a decade: *Libresse oblige* (Editura Crater, 1998), *The Lion Mark* (*Leul Marcu*, Editura Aritmos, 2000), and a volume of selected and new poems, *The Art of Seduction* (*Arta seducţiei*, Editura Vinea, 2002). Ţuţuianu was one of seven poets—and the only woman—featured in a fat anthology of important contemporary Romanian poets, *Manual of Literature* (*Manualul de literatură*, Editura Vinea, 2004).

Ţuţuianu's latest collections of poetry are *Your Magnanimity* (*Mărinimia Ta*, Editura Brumar, 2010—the capitalized "Your," "*Ta*," refers to God, she affirmed to me in an e-mail), and *Sappho*, an anthology of her erotic poems gathered from previous collections spanning her career (Editura Cartea Românească, 2012). Many of the poems in *Sappho* have been translated into English in *Syllables of Flesh*. Ţuţuianu has commented, "Sappho and Emily Dickinson are my favorite poets. I would like to live like Sappho and write like Emily. Or to live like Emily and write like Sappho."

Either way, a kind of religious perspective is conflated with a secular woman's freedom of body and spirit. The Romanian-French poet Linda Maria Baros has characterized Ţuţuianu's lyrical self as "multiform" and "border-crossing," both saint and siren at the same time. To Baros, Ţuţuianu embodies a "primitive androgyny," "the human (the female bust)" united with "the divine ichthus (the fishtail)."

In the poem bearing his name in its title, the apostle Mark turns his leonine head to look benignly at Ţuţuianu, seeming in his guise as emblem to bless the poet's seeking. Indeed, he is irreducibly an iconographic lion, neither church father nor saint, a symbolic creation like Ţuţuianu's own poetic persona. Meanwhile, Ţuţuianu's literary journey continues across a strange, alien landscape. Hers is a contemporary world of textuality, figures of speech and allusions to Greek and Christian mythos, in which apostles, lions, men, flesh, and self are mere traces. These become referents in a body of words that is constructed of, then deconstructs into, a multiplicity of fragments and hints. In the poet's microcosm of texts, the poem is comprised of words that are "stuttering and unsure," resources that are "squandered," "mumbling," and "shameless" as well. In a commensurate dichotomy, the poet is both a sacrificial woman who "throws herself on the flames" and an enduring spirit who though "mere skin and bone . . . survived in just one word."

Such "syllables of flesh"—with "my sex at the word's heart"—bring Lilith and Leda to life, storied women who could not keep their lovers. Under the spell of Țuțuianu's poetry even her hex words, chanted in lines that she chooses to "write on sand," seem to be sexed up; for instance, the names of fourth-century martyrs, Minodora, Mitrodora, Nymphodora, three virgin sisters executed for their faith, whose recitation in "The Lion Mark" is preceded by the three titles of Henry Miller's *Rosy Crucifixion* trilogy, *Nexus, Plexus, Sexus.* These allusions are eclectic, vexing, fantastical, provocative. It should be no wonder that Țuțuianu titled an early collection of her poetry in Romanian "The Art of Seduction." Her poetry's allure is physical, or perhaps I should say carnal, but likewise literary, the achievement of the creator's words.

Ultimately, Floarea Țuțuianu's witchery—the lexical illusion of strength that paradoxically is one and the same with desire and absence—is the enravishing, voluptuous, transformative utterance of a poet-sorceress who was perhaps best described in the words of poet and novelist Ruxandra Cesereanu as "a postmodern succubus."

Syllables of Flesh

Snow White

My red hair left as a keepsake
on a branch with apple blossoms
a cloud of petals shook
queen bees—over me—
until I was mantled in white

Of late I'm again white—therefore—pure

Fear took its first steps
the speed with which it grew
threatened to reach beyond my shoulders

Could somebody (a poet)
or something (a poem)
still make me white in just one breath?

I dig my nails into the poem's flesh
until it bleeds
and no word gushes forth

Endless Sunday

Between window and wall
sitting in bright sunlight
on this endless Sunday
I cast out of myself
everything that's good everything that's bad

Today I trample myself underfoot
what I had to live—I lived
what I had to lose—I lost

Today I lick my wounds—my verses
All day long I'll balance a poem in the air with my gaze
until exhausted we both collapse

On this endless Sunday
in bright sunlight
sitting by the wall

Thick White Piqué Dress

My life in poetry
(sometimes on Sunday before the mirror)
will dress in the thick white piqué dress
of Emily Dickinson

And because it is shadowed by so many qualities
then—remaining solitary
(before the mirror for twenty-six years)
"Time does go on"

From my ivory apartment tower
on the rope of an illusion I converse
in signs with deaf-mute reality
"Pain—has an Element of Blank—
It cannot recollect"

Soft carpets your feet sink into
line the auricle of your ears
Only sound and fury penetrate
the waves with light an octave higher

I am a she without an oeuvre and she
an Elizabeth Barrett-Browning without a husband

"The brain wider than the sky"—my life
in poetry

The Studio

I sit for hours
in front of the easel

until my face—leaf by leaf—

sticks to the canvas—layer of skin after layer

until the canvas turns into a towel
beads of blood

Look at the face—but what of the likeness?

The Mirror

This mirror no longer recognizes me
it laughs a laugh not mine

Whenever my thirsty neck feels
the imperious necessity of a rope's presence
another sunny day happens by
to put an end to the prospect
each time deferred until some future day
with the smell of a wet dog
On days it drizzles softly
because I'm sadder
I sell myself more dearly
Slender and thinking like a reed
I wrote, for better or worse, a poem
beyond the age limit

This mirror laughs a laugh
not mine

Oglinda

Oglinda aceasta nu mă mai recunoaşte
râde cu un râs care nu e al meu

De câte ori gâtul însetat simte ca
imperios necesară prezenţa unei funii
încă o zi cu soare vine să pună
capăt întâmplării
(de fiecare dată amânată pentru o zi
cu miros de câine ud)
În zilele când plouă mărunt
pentru că sunt mai tristă
mă şi vând mai scump
Suavă şi gânditoare ca o trestie
am scris (de bine de rău) un poem
cu limita de vârstă depăşită

Oglinda aceasta râde cu un râs
care nu e al meu

K.O.

Whenever I'm down
to listen to the grass grow
an angel with a veiled face
counts to ten
the mulberries of my childhood, my Pioneer's tie,
my puberty, my platonic love,
La Princesse de Clèves, almost 8½
Night falls, it's after nine...
A voice from the wings whispers to me,
"Arise and walk"
I try to cling to time
in the adverb "still"
But the eye sinks deep in its socket
less and less light gets through
the skin shows signs of wanting to shrivel
From the heavens above I see myself as small and alone
at a crossroads or in crosswinds
A thin layer of white dust sifts onto my shoulders
I stand on three legs
the smile of the sphinx drowned on my lips:

"I have but the power to kill,
Without—the power to die"—Emily

Delphi—June 1992

Crossing Reality

It's Monday,
and from the kiosk on the corner
a croissant and a new poet under my arm
I start my Dublinesque odyssey

Today I leave imprints in the asphalt

This is the day when I take my face
for a walk past this city's shops
trembling, their windows stare back at me
This is the day when I and myself
go out together for a meal in town, standing

I carry with me a poem born in the metro
angels with haloes huffed from *aurolac* prayed for us
Careful as I usually am
I cross the street the poem on my lips
A car puts the brakes on reality
at my dreaming feet

"Hey, you, monthly poet
rapt in an illusion with a part at the back
walking in heels is like walking on water"

Fish Woman

Everything about you is backwards:
thin ankles propping up very large breasts
advertised sex-appeal
packaged with cement-like frigidity
I have a sense of humor
I have a great many men
whom I keep at arm's length
Most of them see
a close resemblance
between my neck and a telephone cord
Because I like women
I got my men habituated to them
(they have a thing for Gauguin)
Their heads remain turned the wrong way
We trade bodies
Any normal woman should
end better
(not in a fishtail)

My scales cling to them for a long time
stuck to the brain

The Dalles Gallery

I stand face to face with my future
and it tells me nothing. In white knee-highs
the past recedes farther away
with the wave of a red Pioneer's neckerchief
It starts to rain, I fold it neatly
put it on my chest under my shirt
Between the lifeline in my palm
that augurs a bright future
and the rest of life as lived (obligatory life)
a nightmare is born:
you were speaking to Gabriel
in front of the Dalles Gallery and he replied
with a stream of blood from his mouth

At five in the morning
the street cleaners come
dragging their hoses
from the throats of which
gush streams
of blood to cleanse the city
cleaning ironing folding
—no trace of heroes—

....

"And then a Plank in Reason, broke
And I dropped down, and down"

Again you raise your hand to your temple
and memory stains red

In the middle of the street,
kneeling, Gabriel
lights a flower in the snow

The Woman with Feathers

I try to be normal
I mingle with people in the street
I speak loudly, I laugh
I'm a fanatic for fashion
I wait in line patiently
I pay my phone bill
I keep my eyes glued to the shop windows
"She's got traces of feathers on her body
she can fly"
I get lost in the crowd
it's pleasant, warm, with human smells
I carry bags of groceries:
cauliflowers, quinces, chrysanthemums
my mind dwells on a Dutch still life
"She's transparent—she's leading a dead man on foot"
Lazy as I am I still manage
a verse: *whoever is different shall die*
"Get her,
otherwise the slick of sadness she trails behind her will kill us"

Femeia cu pene

Încerc să fiu normală
m-amestec cu lumea pe stradă
vorbesc tare, râd
mă dau în vânt după modă
m-așez cuminte la coadă
plătesc telefonul
lipesc priviri de vitrine
„Are urme de pene pe corp
e-n stare să zboare“
Mă pierd în mulțime
e plăcut, e cald, mirosuri umane
car plasa cu verdețuri:
conopide, gutui, crizanteme
(mi-e gândul la o natură moartă olandeză)
„E transparentă–duce un mort pe picioare“
Leneșă cum sunt las să-mi scape
un vers: *cine se deosebește piere*
„Prindeți-o
altfel dâra tristeții lăsată de ea ne omoară“

An Eye for an Eye and Art for Art's Sake

If we had met
we would have killed each other with a glance
(an eye for an eye and art for art's sake)
My head on a tray cut off by a verse
Your bleeding body sketched on paper

Metamorphosis

I sharpen myself and come to a crisis like class struggle
Short hairy legs support a swollen body
ending in knotty hands

I move with difficulty

I'm a large insect that climbs walls
Colors like dried bird droppings
block the doorway
The floor is heaped with
crumpled paper
"This is my letter to the world
That never wrote to me—"
From the ceiling Franz looks puny,
bent over his writing desk
Emily takes smaller and smaller steps
between bed and window
Today's the day I pluck
the hairs sprouting from my chin
The birth of a line is foretold
every time by a stench

I've grown
a multitude of breasts instead of dresser drawers

A Constipated Day

There are days when the sky settles so low
it presses on your brain
It's a constipated day
Black birds hang suspended
in thick milky air

From a small pile of ashes
you must be reborn every day
without anybody blowing
over your face the least illusion
you can use as a crutch
to get from the bed to the writing desk
from the writing desk to the window

Outside the city awaits you (without you it's dead)
You have to carry it on your back
Solemn and stiff, your feet wet
you'll traverse it from end to end
On your right a row of street dogs
On your left a row of glue-sniffers
signs hanging from their necks
and halos tied with string
kissing your clothes

Night falls. I return, mostly consumed by flames
The city has stolen through the window into my house

Still Life with Mackerel

I was an appetizing
jam, perfect for spreading
on bread
Slender ankles legs crossed
I promised a future luminous
if not blinding
I went about *en pointe*
Each day was stepped on
with frenzy candor and color
We were the three graces of the same idol
the virgin woman the fish woman the rope woman
Each leaves a bit of herself
for the final one—the cannon woman
When our idol got drunk
we changed from models—to artists
On the horizon the future kept shrinking
(it could barely be seen)
in the meantime it changed to the past

Now I'm a lemon
I'm pale and yellow
Only when I look at you
is my soul set on edge—
there's nothing left to squeeze

From a fish woman I've become a mackerel
I've gained flesh and suffering
From time to time a wave tosses me
on the shore and into a still life

The Man and the Flower

The expected one came
his face bathed in light
and I let him go

The unwanted one came and I gave him
body and blood, bread and salt
A thought shot like a bullet through his brain:
"You have used me as a man"
And he turned his face from me

I withered
the candy-sweet rose became a pressed flower
I lost petal after petal
I no longer expected anything. When
there appeared a sort of man. Skinny
(he had one less rib)
"This is how I am"
"Yes. I am the true one"

I've carried this scent inside me since you were born

This Is My Body

This is my body—head in the clouds
bearing traces of kisses and cuneiform
If you scrape it with your nail
a thigh is revealed, long forgotten
traces of holy oil, bread and salt
Share it out in twelve lonelinesses
for this secret meeting
Each loneliness will bear
its own cross, surely
at the dividing of night from day
until the crown of thorns bursts into bloom

Each sin blooms as a wound

This is my body—beads of blood and dew—
whose swan song
I am

Acesta este trupul meu

Acesta este trupul meu (cu capul în nori)
poartă urme de săruturi și litere cuneiforme
Dacă scrijelești cu unghia
apare o coapsă (uitată de mult)
urme de mir, pâine și sare
Împărțiți-l în douăsprezece singurătăți
pentru această întâlnire de taină
Fiecare singurătate își va purta
crucea până când probabil
(la despărțirea nopții de zi)
va înflori cununa de spini

(Fiecare păcat înflorește într-o rană)

Acesta îmi este trupul–broboane de sânge și rouă–
al cărui cântec de lebădă
Sunt

La femme poison

Tarted up
and dragged down by thought
secretly polishing a solitude of dreams
Yes. I'm a body who flings herself at words

The fresh smell of paper, ink
makes me giddy. When I read
I can multiply by means of spores

Pencil in my hand I caress you
and take your breath away
so flower-like yet carnivorous

Even now you won't leave me
with my face washed by words on the knife-
edge of the tongue—
when the last verse loses its way

Self-Portrait with Chimera

It took its time
its shadow before it
trampling it on all fours

Its face looked like a vestal virgin's
half was in the light—
it had a sensuous mouth with a snake's
tongue, slanted nostrils and an eye
whose gaze charred everything it looked upon
The other half of the face was
deep in shadow—a gorgon lost in thought

It had a woman's stride and a cat's gait
its nut-like sex was covered
by neither hand nor hair
but by a lion's tail or a snake's
It smelled of fetid woman
freshly-possessed female

I'd have liked it beside me to get to know it
it stretched out on its belly, its face in the dust
I stretched out on my back, my face in the light
to have chatted together:
how it swallowed like swords scores of men
who didn't know what to answer—
how I gave myself to old King David
and how—nobody could touch me since then—
and other trifles...

But without warning it opened its eagle's
wings unnoticed before then
let its shadow cover me and flew
like a thought in sunlight

I'm a Swamp

An absolute mess
Lycra stockings with garters bras and bikinis
(forms without content)—tossed on the rug
ah, this lingerie full of
memories (contour without form)
emotions and resentments vacillating between
acrid-sacred sweat and profane perfume
I'm a swamp:
my bed keeps my body's form
the sheet I walk in from poem
to poem—my devoted dog
I wash it once in a while wring it out hang it to dry:
"you'll have to throw away something of yourself
to be a perfect mimic a subtle cheat
you'll need a straw to take sips
from the young poets and their latest books
you'd give anything to be convincing"
this impulse lasts only
a moment—for meanwhile the strophe wrinkles
gets tossed in the waste basket

I'm a swamp:
I don't know how to measure time
it could be February or November: both
seasons reveal the same landscape glued outside the window—
gray sky bare branches
And the hour hides from me according to the darkness
inside, outside it could be six in the morning
when objects begin to take on contour

or six in the evening
when objects begin to lose contour

At odd moments sharp pain and cold
in the brain spine womb
beads of blood on the forehead—

It tests me. The poem.
Now when I've lost my maternal instincts

Narcissa Is My Flower Name

From time to time
I hug my shoulders with my hands
my elbows cover my chest
I sit in the lotus position
my ankles cover my sex
I caress myself in my mind just to caress myself
and I say to myself, I'm easy, a light woman
who can rise to a height
where nobody might touch me
(what you assume about an undine resides inside)

If no one else can be found
I must love myself
I lean over the floor and it turns into a mirror
I want to kiss my reflection
the whisper of a breeze stirs ripples
I test the water-mirror with a toe
and plunge into it along with my reflection

The floor blooms in a blood stain

Hotline

Gaze dangling at one end of the phone cord—
a cord that stretches from bed to shower
and from shower to rug—umbilical cord
between loneliness and a voice from the wings

My gingerbread heart
falls backwards like a shot at its sound
a bit of *feeling,* diazepam—the evening drug
a kiss on the forehead before going to bed
Sometimes I smother its sound with the pillow
delaying loneliness until later
posing in my negligee on high heels

A black-and-white life in a gray apartment house
whispered tenderly on the tip of the tongue
making eights in the receiver
becomes *la vie en rose, la vie en bonbon*
life sipped like champagne
from a slipper

I'm a light and transparent woman
if I stand where it's bright you can read through me
It's the place from which
without seeing, without smelling, without touching
I can either put in chains or put to rout

Sexy(Oxy)moron

In the beginning she was a woman with legs on her shoulders

She took his head in her hands and flipped him upside-down
took his lips with her fingers then blew kisses
and thrust her tongue into his ears until
steaming him up—words were loosed

Her body winked at him with an inward eye

Oh he watched her through verses Oh passed her from light
to thought's shadow Oh fixed her between his eyelashes and
Oh with eternal sadness penetrated her Oh in the fiery zero
between two words—(w)hole(ly)
and could not save himself

As the text kept throbbing
holy   wholly   holey   holy
the body withdrew exhausted from between the words

In the end he was a man with head fallen
silent in a perfect language

They had heaven on their soles
and the taste of earth on their tongues

I and the Other Part of Me

When the humble part of me licks
words and rhymes from the floor with its tongue
the other part of me anything-goes and naked underneath
crosses her legs
allowing a glimpse of *basic instinct*

While night after night the object part of me
gets into bed as if into a wall
smothered by the pillow of dreams
the other part leans forward slightly to let
the line between her breasts show
the shape of a snake's tongue

Shameless, one part of me
grows older by the cruel light of day
without my being able to stop her
while the frivolous part goes cruising
late-night bars indulgently dishing out
wrinkles on high heels

When I and my guardian angel awaken
to life in the morning and start over
disgustedly the exhausted part of me
gets ready for sleep in the next world

Saint Francis and Clare

From below, the forest and the city seemed ablaze

As I approached there was only the light of the sun
setting blood red
Two silhouettes appeared in a green space
kneeling face to face
between them a white towel laid for a meal
Every kind of bird pecked from their palms
crumbs of thought

Saint Francis took her hand and placed it
on the crown of his tonsured head—undressing her with his gaze
she felt the chill of his gaze on her body—
"beyond all gifts is that of
conquering yourself"
At the very moment he dressed her again
Clare felt the warmth of his gaze enveloping her anew

They ate though touching
nothing, with a gentle breath Saint Francis
raised her in the air, she felt as if she were floating
for an instant, then he carefully set her back down

Smoothing the creases in her skirt she thanked him in her mind
for his miraculous gift: this UN-NOTHINGNESS beyond bounds
un-happened between them

The forest and the city remained ablaze—
especially at night—in their gaze

Assisi, June 1997

Saint Francis and Clare (The Supplicants)

Holding her head between his knees and
cutting her hair (fallen to his feet)
he felt in his hand a splendid cranium
with virgin thorns

When with his lips he caught
the nipple of the grape
the roof of his mouth glistened with the milky way
—perfuming it

Pierced—the earthen-hued sackcloth
an *oh* passed through the needle's slit and
stopped in the eardrum—
tingling

Assisi, June 1997

The Promise like a Certainty

Like an immense sun blazing lassitude
and helplessness as it rotates on its axis
a long time ago you stopped being a promise
like life
you became a certainty like death,
he told me, tracing his finger
from my heart to the hollow
between the two collarbones
trying to feel the spot where
the soul flies free

Between the first poem that deflowered me
and the last poem that I abandoned
all my lovers have remained
wordless

Everything I touch turns to poetry
I have a hand of gold
that could bury me alive

Promisiunea ca o certitudine

Ca un imens soare lenea strălucitoare
şi neputinţa învârtindu-se în jurul axei sale
Tu nu mai eşti de mult o promisiune
precum viaţa
Ai devenit o certitudine precum moartea
Îmi spuse el plimbându-şi degetul
de pe inimă spre scobitura
dintre cele două clavicule
încercând să găsească locul prin care
iese sufletul

Între primul vers care m-a deflorat
şi ultimul vers abandonat
toţi iubiţii mei au rămas fără
de cuvinte

Tot ce ating se transformă în poezie
am o mână de aur
care ar putea să mă îngroape de vie

Amor fati

At birth I received a white crown
made of cute little lonelinesses
(who would have suspected that loneliness
grows plump over time)

Later scores of men came to deposit
their love-offerings at my feet
some I trampled on (I paid for this afterward)
others I left for women
more fragile weak lonesome
than I
I was preoccupied with turning my fate around
I alone could accomplish this
I was waiting for a sign from on high
sent especially for me

"Waiting is the gift God
bestowed on me—I wait so beautifully it would be
a pity if anything happened"

Years later we met in the street—they (couples)
were a single body with many eyes but
only one tongue
I—airy and translucent, taking lessons
in levitation with my hands hidden behind my back
full of lines of poetry and wrinkles
We were surprised how thoroughly the weather
had worked us over
We each went our own way on the high wire toward our fate

half of me carrying loneliness
like a white lamb across my shoulders

Before I Die I'll Go Sleep a While

I sleep on half the bed, the other half
is empty black and deep with damp sheets

I sleep on my right side curled slightly
my hands between my knees keeping vigil
on the self torn between ego and superego
squeezing the hot sheets between my thighs
beyond good and evil

In dream, death traces a fingernail along the curve
of my spine: I sweat. Goose bumps
creep down my arms my hands. The color
drains from my face. Settles in my legs. I'm white
as whitewash. I laugh with my mouth on the back of my head

Desperate I feel the poem and recognize it
line by line. In my sleep I make the sign of the cross with my tongue
That it save me: the Word in the sky of my mouth
could save me if it would

Like a Rare Bird

She hops to the tip of the tongue
not to disturb the remnant of tomorrows
A nude exhausting a mirror—
body set loose in words
Light settled in layers on her forehead
                a crown of thorns and laurels—
                the dust of words

And soon I'll die like a rare bird
on my own tongue

The Lion Mark

Every morning a woman
slips out of a man's skin and throws herself on the flames
I no longer know what I look like
here where the eye rolls in complete circles not seeing itself
here where the sand makes you one with the earth that fills you
I write on sand: *Nexus Plexus Sexus*
Minodora Mitrodora Nymphodora until
the sand flies away helter-skelter (And I . . . a line furrowing the sand)
I'm flat on the ground I tell myself pressing my face to its surface
mumbling shameless words through nose and mouth
I'll have to prepare a word with flesh of my flesh
and blood of my blood
He is going to fill me. This word will be my soul
I'll give birth to him through my mouth.
I stand up, stumble in my wings

Over his shoulder the Lion Mark gazes at me with meek yellow eyes

Nonnus

Look Nonnus
the sand collects in me day after day grain by grain for years on end

Between you and me: it's been a long time since I made waves
No longer do I felt cloth out of my fishtail scales shaken free
The sailors smelled me many miles away
and fried me in another story...
Look I told you the sand collects in me
and from one day to the next I become *another*
more or less woman
until the final woman inside me on whom the dust settles
in a heap
All my life you sweet-talked me by the hand but here and now

I'll tear out the word's meaning by mouth
                    The rest we shall bless in silence

Leda and the Swan

I laughed cut loose turned cartwheels
I invented men of paper
from paper head to paper toe eyes bulging with words

I laughed squandered words
until mere skin and bone I survived in just one word

I threw that word high in the air
Then a shower of gold fecundated the poet in me
while on the wall I drew the shadow of my sex

The lunatic the virgin the man poked their heads out
They breathed fire through their mouths at the stroke of each hour

Oh Lord God, let me stay woman
I want to be Leda, the swan between my legs

A Flower in the Lions' Den

You should put a price on my head so I won't lose it
for a part of me finds herself thrown in the den
where the lions of my sign await me

Face to face eyeball to eyeball with God

"I found woman more bitter than death"
and for this you should put...

I have put stone upon stone a pyramid of books
the price of a life here and everywhere word after word
until no more were left. But it came to pass

Look at me alive in your sleeping eyes

He's the One

The cage of my chest
is a most beautiful display window through which he watches
and is watched (people see him living then dying)

He's the first among men
who reaches me with his thought walking on water

My breasts are in his hands
and with them he divides the waters from the land
the word from a sign

For him I have (set aside) a great emptiness in my stomach
that catches in his throat when he sees me coming or going

In good times and bad he is my fish on dry land
who enters me first with the tip and then with plenitude

A Kingdom for a Man

Little nightmares nip at me
I'm sitting on a thousand and one needles. The sand eddies
silver scales glisten in the soil
                    I see snake-woman

An angel comes and goes comes and goes. Bends above
a siren who hardly can breathe through her bronchi
but who covers her hand with her sex (her sex-shell)
                    I see fish-woman

A kingdom. For a man

Nothing can be compared to the dew of his brow
the drops upon my lips while he sweated above me

Oh, Nonnus, it's not for you to understand but for the gods
to applaud me

Pentacle of Love

I remember his tongue he had a mouth of gold
that piously spun the word in me. Powerful
Make me bounden to your word

His eye slithering downward fixed itself upon my foot
I had to tread on it wherever I went. Farther
May your mercy be. A gift

My eyes met their end according to the words or saying,
When you caress me, pierce my body with your fear
Ever-patient my heart expanded and gave forth
the mustard seed like a mountain. A walking mountain
I was his early fruit. The toil of years. Worth it.

Glorify and Leap

Look, you have me, a woman, and peer over my shoulders
    into the book
You want me on paper in the glare of daylight
to take a man from head to toe
    at only the exclamation mark (!)
after the same man takes you to the tips of your fingernails
    at only the question mark (?)
I'm all words. But. Talk smells of deeds:
the pleasure of licking your lips
after you've swallowed so many failures that taste of victory
the last will be the first or even worse
    Can it be true
you think that my traces in the desert are erased signs?
Every day the light measures my shadow growing/shrinking
The sky leans on me. God is above. Push
    Stand at my right so I don't totter
A blind thought both deaf and dumb stubbornly follows my traces
    Glorify and leap
on the seventh day you'll be one death richer

Preamărește și saltă

Uite, mă ai ca femeie și te uiți peste umerii mei
    în carte
Mă vrei pe hârtie în plină amiază
A lua un bărbat din tălpi până-n creștet
    doar la semnul mirării (!)
După ce același bărbat te ia până-n vârful unghiilor
    doar la semnul întrebării (?)
Numai gura e de mine. Dar. Gura miroase a fapte:
plăcerea de-a te linge pe buze
după ce-ai înghițit atâtea eșecuri cu gust de victorii
cei din urmă vor fi cei dintâi sau mai rău
    Adevărat,
urmele mele-n deșert sunt pentru tine semn spulberat?
Cu fiecare zi lumina îmi măsoară umbra în (des)creștere
Cerul se lasă pe mine. Dumnezeu e deasupra. Apasă
    Stai de-a dreapta mea ca să nu mă clatin
Un gând orb și mut și surd stă neclintit pe urmele mele:
    Preamărește și saltă
că în ziua a șaptea vei fi mai bogată cu-o moarte

My Dog—the Soul

Hand over my heart I pledge the oath
under my tongue the word fermenting in saliva—solitary
under the mouth's sky

In my ear life whispers the salt sea
Green and dry are the words from which I hang
upside down

I see from far off how I blanch white then closer ever closer

Immeasurable the goodness according to which Emmanuel
weighs heavy on
my dog—the soul

The white glare of the word will reflect all colors
until the last glint

I had no choice. I was chosen.

Not my body, not my soul, but my sex at the word's heart
my strong point

The Glory of Four Walls

Once again I prowl around the glory enclosed in four walls

I circle them
Scratch with my fingernail. My tongue licks worn whitewash
I wear their corners round, day and night. Always

At each corner I wait

They take a step toward me. Then they stop
Another step. Again they stop
Lately they advance even while I watch
Lately they advance. Even while

Soon their loneliness will overtake me
Soon loneliness will pulse in my blood

The beast in me catches the scent. Completely subjugates me
The fear in me submits. We climb the walls
The ceiling blocks us (the leap)

What a plunge. Out of nowhere. Words cringe. Bark at me

From Sun to Shade

Like an immense street silent hot and empty
I languish between the apartments on a Sunday afternoon
I suffer with the asphalt from one end to the other
My stiletto heels leave impressions in me

Like an emaciated bitch in a dream
I slink after the word from sun to shade

ALMANACH. POV
L'AN DE GRACE M.DC. XXX

Lilith

Stuttering and unsure of itself
each verse of mine ends in you
A hundred verses make a river that flows
into your oceanic dead love
then return against me

We are made of dust for one another
and with the sweat of our brains shall we love one another
until one of us gains the day

Then you must choose the woman from the sowing of your ribs
that out of her thighs syllables of flesh may bloom
henceforth your buried name shall be handed down
from generation to generation

I'm betting on dust
I remain your equal in solitude

Lilith

Gângav și nesigur pe el
fiecare vers al meu se termină-n tine
O sută de versuri fac un fluviu care se varsă în
marea ta dragoste moartă apoi se întorc
împotrivă-mi

Suntem făcuți (din țărână) unul pentru celălalt
și cu sudoarea minții ne vom iubi până când
care pe care va dobândi

Iar tu îți vei alege femeie din seminția coastelor tale
ca dintre coapsele ei să iasă silabe de carne
astfel ca numele tău îngropat să fie dus
din neam în neam mai departe

Eu mizez pe țărână
Eu rămân egala ta întru singurătate

He Hasn't Yet Been Born

He hasn't yet been born
the man who could be half what I am as a woman

Even if they weep between my thighs
my lovers are the good old boys of other women
Together we make paper children whom we raise with zeal
When we get bored we fold them into airplanes
because it's endless and tiring for the body
to read books

You can't take a man from another woman's mouth

Wasted on page after page their seed swells my books

Pale I feel the tree of life rustling through them

Their smiles I cut myself on each morning
The blood I bathe in each night
because love is as indomitable as death
tramp tramp tramping toward life

He hasn't yet been born
the man who could be half what I am as a woman

The Art of Seduction

Ear doesn't hear me. Eye sees what it believes
Tongue doesn't obey. Time is against me

Somebody comes leafs through me goes away. Somebody else comes
tramples me waits. The last to come
shall also be the first who
puts a finger on his tongue then riffles through me
page by page: only sophisticated words with a model's legs
He sees in color and everything moves. Let him lead us on

I prolong it through words. Only milk and honey
He squeezes me between pages. He wants to know much more
I pour a little poison. Just enough. I bathe it in words
I stay on his brain on his tongue. I spew fire and pearls
from my mouth
Loneliness is transmitted from me through oral contact
He turns pensive. Sees blue. Becomes other
Wants to capture me alive. Skin me
I scream discreetly disappear with easy elegance between the lines

Ear doesn't hear me. Eye sees what it believes
Tongue doesn't obey. Time is against me

Will Be or Won't Be at All

He who loves his woman
loves himself and his own limbs
Silent as a fish the sex breathes. Heat

He is ahead of everyone and everything
through him in me I'm at the end of patience. Sitting

I yearn to separate from the body
to be in one soul with J. deeply needing one another
for a good aroma. In one scent

Bounded by boundlessness
He is in me but has yet to touch me
My lover will be or won't be at all. Religious

Man the Altar and Woman the Transept

If I shed my first skin soft and velvet
and my second with scales and quills
If I shed my thoughts shameless and naked
seventy-times-seven times
down to the blood down to the bone
Will the rood-screen still separate man the altar
from woman the transept?
A snail circumnavigates the globe on me
from head to toe
and leaves a sticky track that feels warm
the trace of a fish in water of a bird in air
and of man in woman
For the crazy thought that crosses my mind
I must touch the ground with my knees, forehead
and parched chapped lips
seventy-times-seven times

Nonnus, raise me up to the power of your highness, I pray!

I'm the One Who

Sometimes a double-edged word
slips between my shadow and me

I lick my boredom out of my palms just can't get enough
Inexhaustible source of smells I'll drown in my own juice

I'm ever more filled and rippled by my senses
the sand doesn't swallow me the paper doesn't hold me

I clap air
I catch the word in flight I walk it to and fro
Then I place it under a sword with double meaning

One of us will reign over a great disquiet

Sightless I Gazed on Death's Face

I'd left behind
a gaze summoning love I passed beyond the seventh heaven
I became a sphere covered by wings
that pierced my eyes like blinding arrows

You gave me birth I carried you in my arms
then I urged you to learn to walk—lean on me
take your last steps toward God

I was scattered over the ground I was made of earth I couldn't
put myself together again I couldn't take solid form

Inside me you struggled to get free
I clung to you tightly so you'd have to stay

The image drew its fear upon its face

Your gaze passed beyond me far beyond
it was suspended in the GREAT VOID

And there was light in your darkness

Brain grew thorns and heart bled among them
I saw death with my father's closed eyes
God is great. God is good.
But he got stuck in my throat I can't swallow him
O Lord without you I'm no one's

I'd left behind
a gaze summoning love I passed beyond the seventh heaven
I became a sphere covered by wings
that pierced my eyes like blinding arrows

I was You. You were God among us

Rejoice

Rejoice,
you'll wander alone across the Word from one end to the other

Like a gust of wind
a double-edged lily sails through your soul
Only your swan's neck, a swan who swallowed her own song
only she knows how—you'll have to stretch it high

The eye cleansing itself
all words poor in sadness have gone to the dogs
Rejoice for the one who is going to look behind him—and lose you

O sleeper
light as a snowflake you'll be raised aloft on mounds of flowers
You'll be the first to set foot in heaven.
It's all yours. Adam and Adama.
Earth flows out of him

Rejoice,
this is the land where the Word alone will grace you
The Song of Songs, The Holy of Holies, The Book of the Dead.

The Book of Life

I need my sleep
Only in sleep does the poetry I have to write
yield itself to me

Between the two of us there's a book
we make our way through it while we live
Its pages rustle like my skin
as your lips learn to read it

It's alive, I tell you:
the words live in a secret language
If you rest your ear against it
soul water and blood begin to speak

It's a book lived in full exactly as written:
in a life read all in one breath

Your Name

I fought with you all night long
oh that you could be cold or hot
but you're neither cold nor hot
you pass through me leaving only a trace
that points of course toward the thighs

The letter brings death and the spirit gives life
but the one within finds renewal day by day
with light's lint snagged between the eyelashes
in the early morning. What is your name?

True, my passing through you leaves a mark
(a book written inside in reverse)
He who holds his soul dear will lose it

You're not the first or the last
but you're the only one who after this night
bears my name on his forehead and my name
is wonderful

About the Author

Floarea Țuțuianu ["Tsu-tsu-ya'-nu"] graduated from the Nicolae Grigorescu Institute of the Fine Arts in Bucharest and turned to publishing poetry after the Romanian revolution at the end of 1989. She has published six books of poetry: *The Fish Woman* (*Femeia pește*, Editura Cartea Românească, 1996); *Libresse oblige* (Editura Crater, 1998); *The Lion Mark* (*Leul Marcu*, Editura Aritmos, 2000); a volume of selected and new poems, *The Art of Seduction* (*Arta seducției*, Editura Vinea, 2002); and *Your Magnanimity* (*Mărinimia Ta*, Editura Brumar, 2010). Recently, she compiled an anthology of her erotic poetry gathered from previous collections throughout her career, *Sappho* (Editura Cartea Românească, 2012).

Țuțuianu has commented, "Sappho and Emily Dickinson are my favorite poets. I would like to live like Sappho and write like Emily. Or to live like Emily and write like Sappho."

Țuțuianu is a graphic designer at the Romanian Cultural Institute Publishing House in Bucharest, where she lives. She continues to work as a visual artist as well as a poet, and her numerous exhibits have appeared not only in Romania but also in Greece, France, Italy, Turkey, Israel, England, Holland, Germany, and Austria.

In 2011, Adam J. Sorkin and Irma Giannetti published *My Dog—the Soul/Câinele meu—sufletul*, a dozen poems in a dual-language chapbook published in New Zealand from Cold Hub Press. Țuțuianu's poems in Sorkin's and Giannetti's translations have appeared in notable poetry magazines in the U.S. and the U.K., including *The Marlboro Review, Artful Dodge, Turnrow, Tampa Review, New Letters, Puerto del Sol, 5 AM, Diode,*

Poetry International, Blood Orange Review, Modern Poetry in Translation, St. Petersburg Review, and two anthologies, *The Vanishing Point That Whistles: Contemporary Romanian Poetry*, ed. Paul Doru Mugur, Sorkin and Claudia Serea (Talisman House, 2011), and *Romanian Writers on Writing*, ed. Norman Manea and Sanda Cordoş (Trinity University Press, 2011). Her poetry has also been translated into French, German, Hungarian, Italian, Polish, Czech, and Turkish. In 2007, she was awarded the Poetry Prize of the Lucian Blaga International Poetry Festival.

About the Translators

Adam J. Sorkin has published more than fifty books of translation, and his work has won the Poetry Society (U.K.) Prize for European Poetry Translation as well as the International Quarterly Crossing Boundaries Award, the Kenneth Rexroth Memorial Translation Prize, the Ioan Flora Prize for Poetry Translation, and the Poesis Translation Prize, among others. His recent publications include *A Sharp Double-Edged Luxury Object* by Rodica Draghincescu, translated with Antuza Genescu (Červená Barva Press, 2014); *Gold and Ivy/Aur și iederă* by George Vulturescu, translated with Olimpia Iacob (Eikon, 2014); *The Starry Womb* by Mihail Gălățanu, translated with Petru Iamandi and the author (Diálogos Books, 2014); and *The Book of Anger* by Marta Petreu, translated with Christina Zarifopol-Illias and Liviu Bleoca (Diálogos Books, 2014). *The Hunchback's Bus* by Nora Iuga, translated with Diana Manole, appeared from Bitter Oleander Press in the fall of 2016. *Eclogue* by Ioana Ieronim, translated with the author, is forthcoming from Červená Barva Press. Sorkin is Distinguished Professor of English, Penn State Brandywine.

Irma Giannetti grew up in Cluj-Napoca, in the Transylvania region of Romania, speaking Hungarian and Romanian. She studied English and French as an undergraduate in Romania, then English and Comparative Literature as a graduate student in the United States, including at Penn State. At Penn State University Park, she has worked in technology support and now serves as an adviser in the Division of Undergraduate Studies, an enrollment unit for first- and second-year exploratory students.

Her co-translations with Adam J. Sorkin have appeared widely in literary magazines, as well as in a number of anthologies. Giannetti has also contributed translations of articles from French and Romanian to a special issue of *Dada/Surrealism*, "From Dada to Infra-noir: Dada, Surrealism, and Romania" (2015).

www.ingramcontent.com/pod-product-compliance
Lightning Source LLC
Chambersburg PA
CBHW042338040426
42447CB00018B/3476
9780996072236